A MATHEMATICIAN LIKE me

WRITTEN BY

Dr Shini Somara
WITH Catherine Coe

ILLUSTRATED BY

Nadja Sarell

wren & rook

Oh no! Aliyah overslept, and her cousin's arriving any minute to take her camping. She races around getting dressed super-quickly.

"Hi, Aliyah," Robin says. "Are you ready?"

"Yes! Where are we going?"

"That's a surprise." Robin winks. "First we have to go shopping."

"We have to go to two places," Robin says. "So how many things will we get in each shop?"

Tent pegs
Rope
Fruit
Marshmallows

Aliyah works it out. "There are four different items . . . so two in one shop and two in another. Or three in one and one in the other!"

Robin nods. "Numbers are all around us!"

"I need some new tent pegs because my old ones are bent," Robin says when they get to the first shop.

"Tent pegs need to be straight to keep the rope tight. They must be put in the ground at an angle to grip into the soil, otherwise they'll come out and the tent will fall down!"

"What's an angle?" Aliyah asks.

An angle is the distance between two lines that meet each other. Angles are measured in degrees.

A full circle has 360 degrees ...

and a quarter circle has 90 degrees, which is called a right angle.

45°

45°

Tent pegs need to be at a 45-degree angle from the ground.

Aliyah looks at the list. "We can get rope in here too!"
She grabs the nearest pack of rope, but Robin shakes her head.

"That rope is too thick for the tent poles. We need rope that's four millimetres wide."

"What are millimetres?" Aliyah asks.

"Millimetres are a type of measurement.

There are ten millimetres in a centimetre,

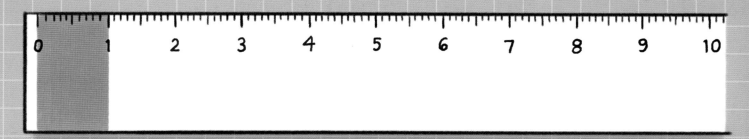

and a hundred centimetres in a metre.

So how many millimetres are in a metre?"

Aliyah thinks hard. "Ten times a hundred … equals a thousand!"

"Correct!" says Robin. "You're good at maths. Like me!"

"Is that your job?"

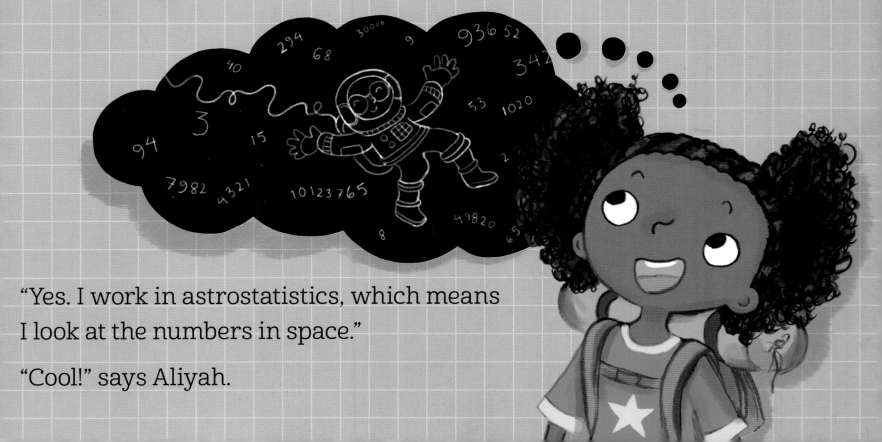

"Yes. I work in astrostatistics, which means
I look at the numbers in space."

"Cool!" says Aliyah.

In the supermarket they go to the fruit aisle.
"What fruit should we take camping?"
Robin asks.

"Oranges?"

"Hmm, they're tasty, but I don't think they'll fit in our
rucksacks! Do you know what their 3D shape is called?"

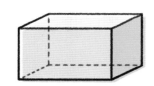   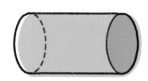   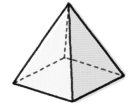

"It's not a cuboid,   or a cylinder,   or a pyramid ..." Aliyah says.

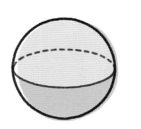   

"It's a sphere!"

Aliyah looks at the different fruit. Most of them are sphere shapes – apples, melons and grapefruit. They're too big and bulky for their bags. Satsumas are spheres too, but they're smaller and can fit in pockets!

"Just one more thing to get now . . ." says Robin. "Marshmallows!"

Aliyah spots a sign when they find the marshmallows.
"What does that mean?" she asks.

Today's offer:

½ price
marshmallows!

"That's a fraction," says Robin. "A fraction is part of a whole number. It can be a good idea to think of fractions as part of a pie."

he bottom number tells you how many equal slices to slice the pie into,

and the top number tells you how many of those slices to have.

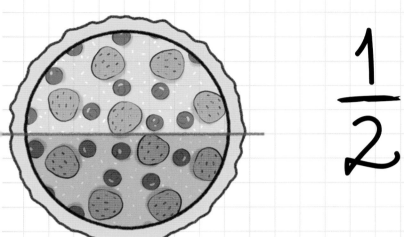

$$\frac{1}{2}$$

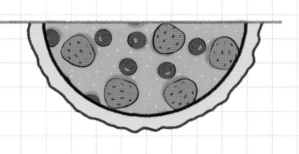

So with 1/2 you slice the pie into two equal pieces and take one of those slices.

"So half the pie?" Aliyah says.

"Yes! The marshmallows are half price, which means we can get two packets for the price of one!"

After they've paid, Aliyah and Robin leave the shop and start walking to the train station.

"We have twenty minutes to get there. That's good. It usually takes ten minutes, but our heavy bags will slow us down today."

"So we can walk half our normal speed and still get there in time?" Aliyah says.

"Exactly!"

"But where are we going?"

"You'll soon see," says Robin. "We need to go twelve stops on the train. If there are five minutes between each stop, how long will the journey be?"

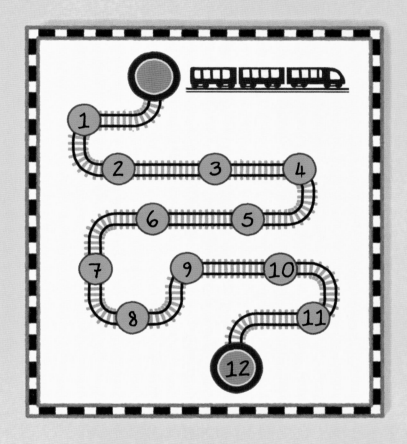

Aliyah frowns. "Can I use the calculator on your phone?"

"Hmmm, calculators are great, but it's good to be able to work out sums ourselves!"

By the time they reach the train station, Aliyah has worked out the sum.

"Ten times by five is fifty and two fives are ten. Fifty plus ten is . . . sixty minutes. Which is the same as an hour!"

See, you don't always need a calculator! But sometimes they can be useful with really big numbers," Robin says.

BLAISE PASCAL invented the first mechanical calculator in 1642, called the Pascaline. The machine had metal wheel dials containing numbers that were turned to create the calculations.

It could add and subtract sums up to five digits. Later Pascal created six-digit and eight-digit versions. He built fifty machines in total!

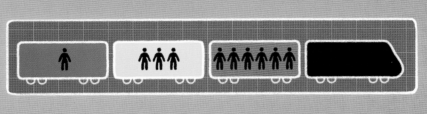

"What's that?" Aliyah asks, pointing at a screen in the train.

"It shows how busy each carriage of the train is so you know where to go to find a seat! Have you heard of Florence Nightingale?"

"She was a nurse, I think? She helped lots of soldiers."

Yes, but that's not all she did. She was also a brilliant mathematician and created charts similar to this one.

When FLORENCE NIGHTINGALE was working in hospitals, she collected data about how clean they were and how this was linked to whether or not the patients recovered.

She published her results, showing how the conditions in a hospital affected the patients, and created the 'coxcomb' chart to show the data. Her work helped save people's lives.

They get off the train at a tiny station. Beside them is a big forest.

Aliyah's jaw drops as they walk towards the trees. "There's so much nature here!"

Robin grins. "Maths is in nature too. Numbers help to make the world more beautiful!"

A man called FIBONACCI loved studying numbers. He discovered a number pattern in nature by looking at how fast rabbits breed.

The Fibonacci sequence starts with 0 and 1, and then the next number is created by adding the previous two numbers together:

0, 1, 1, 2, 3, 5, 8, 13, 21, 34, 55, 89 and so on . . .

Scientists later realised that the numbers in this pattern could be found in many forms of nature, such as the spirals in a pine cone and a seashell.

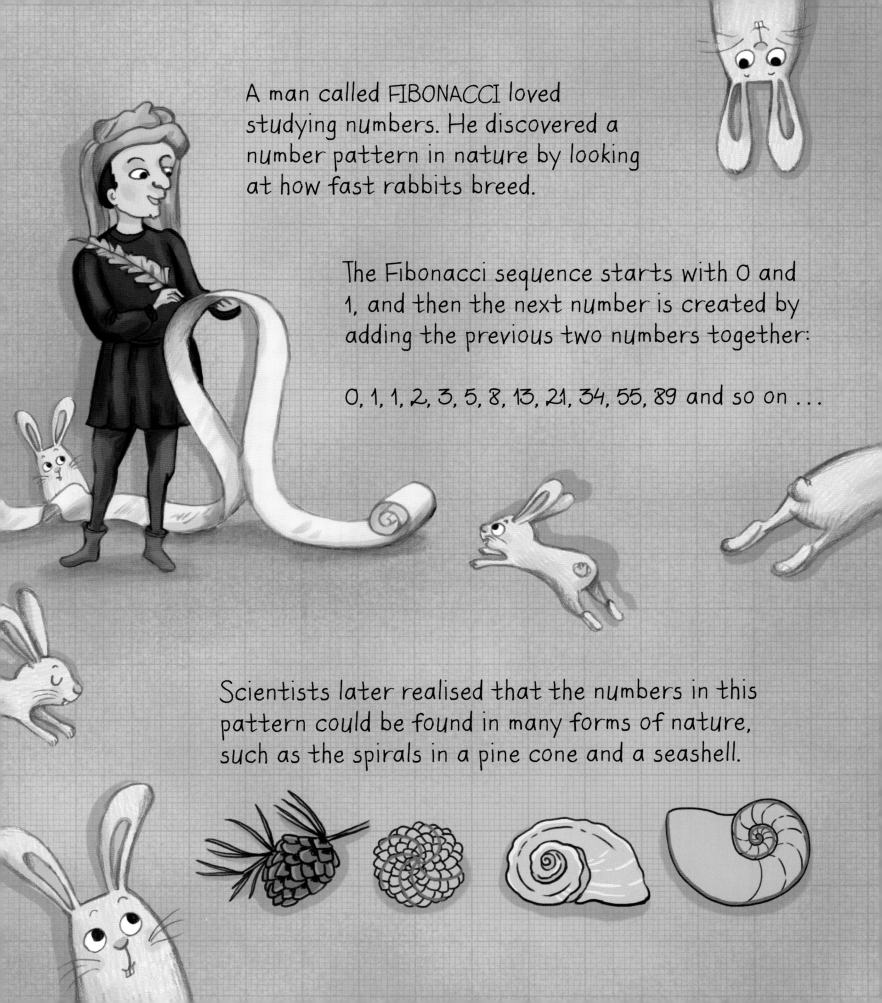

After they've been walking for a while, Robin suddenly stops. "Ta-da! We're here! What do you think?"

Aliyah looks up and up and up … She's never seen trees this high before!

"These trees are called Douglas Firs, and they are some of the tallest in the world. They grow to over 60 metres. That's taller than a space shuttle!"

Douglas Fir

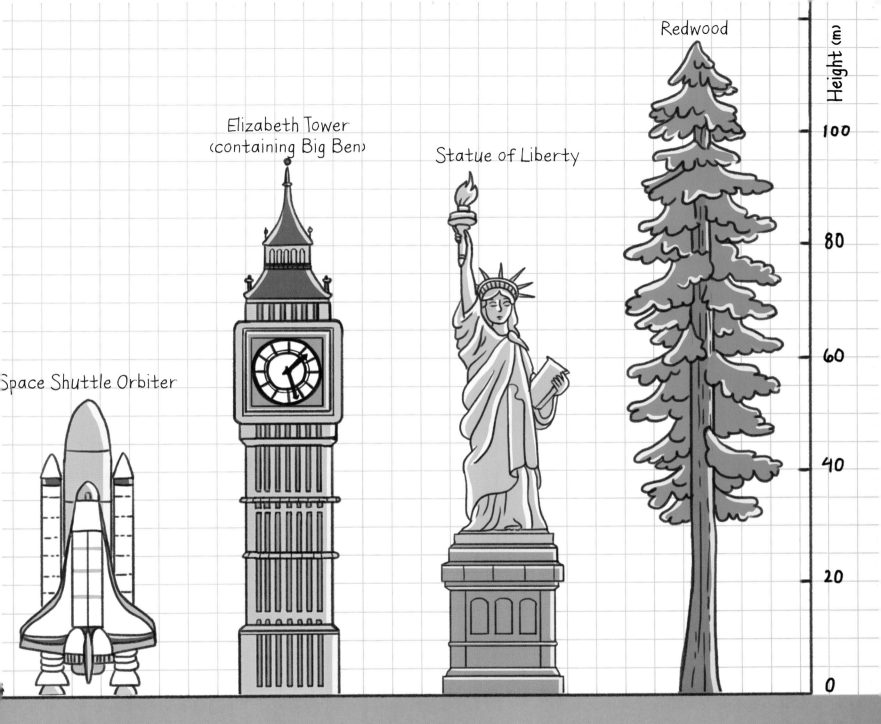

Space Shuttle Orbiter

Elizabeth Tower (containing Big Ben)

Statue of Liberty

Redwood

Height (m)

100

80

60

40

20

0

"Is it taller than Big Ben?" Aliyah asks. "And the Statue of Liberty?"

"I'm afraid not," says Robin. "Big Ben and the Statue of Liberty are close to 100 metres tall. There aren't many trees that grow as tall as that, but the redwood does. The tallest one ever recorded was 116 metres!"

Aliyah and Robin start to set up the tent in a clearing.

"Can you pass me the rope?" Robin asks.

Aliyah tries to throw it to her cousin,
but it doesn't get very far.

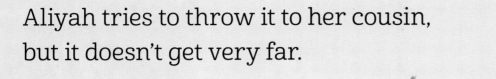

Trajectories are important, especially in space, as you need to know where and how a spacecraft will travel. The mathematician KATHERINE JOHNSON was a leading expert on trajectories, working for NASA.

"Some things have a short trajectory," Robin says. "That's the path that an object takes through the air, and it's another part of maths."

She was responsible for calculating the trajectories for Project Mercury and the Apollo 11 mission. This means she helped Neil Armstrong land on the Moon!

"Look at all the stars!" Aliyah marvels as they toast their marshmallows that night. She's never seen so many before.

"There's maths in stars too. It's used to work out distances between them and also what stars are made of."

CAROLINE HERSCHEL was a mathematician who became the world's first professional female astronomer. Her brother William was King George III's court astronomer and discovered the planet Uranus.

Caroline helped her brother with calculations and the king soon paid her to be William's assistant. In 1786, she became the first woman to discover a comet and spotted seven more comets in her lifetime.

"Wow, maths really is everywhere – even outer space!" Aliyah says, "I just have one more question   "

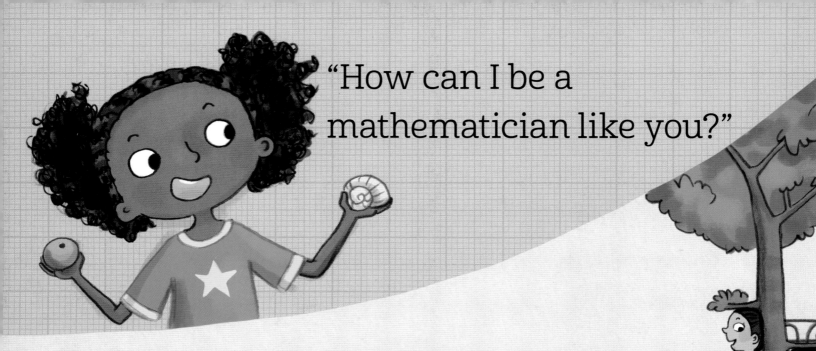

"How can I be a mathematician like you?"

Mathematicians are always trying to understand and improve the world around them by using numbers. They ask lots of questions and look for the answers by spotting patterns and testing their ideas.

You too can use maths every day to find out answers for yourself!

How can you share two oranges with three friends?

How many days until your next birthday?

How many steps does it take to cross the school playground?

How long does it take you to walk to school?

Can you sort your toys by size or shape?

Mathematicians help us solve all kinds of problems big and small. If you like finding solutions, then being good with numbers will really help!

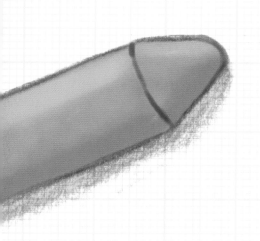

How can I become good with numbers?

We all use maths every day. We use numbers to count things and money, estimate times and measure a variety of different shapes. You can have fun with maths too. Try this game with some friends and see if you can work out the answers!

Draw a big circle on the ground with chalk and divide it into quarters. In each quarter of your circle write: double it, halve it, add five and minus three.

Double it | Halve it

Add five | Minus three

Write a selection of random numbers on pieces of paper. Fold them up so you can't see them and place the numbers in a bowl.

Take it in turns to choose a secret number.

Choose a soft toy which you can throw onto your circle. Then see if you can complete the challenge it lands on, such as doubling your secret number.

Sometimes we don't get the answer right the first time, but that's okay! We can learn from our mistakes.

Double it

Halve it

Add five

Minus three

This book is dedicated to Mum, Dad, Soraya
and especially Sharlene, whose innate gift
for maths was the inspiration for this book.
Thanks to you all for your support and love – S.S.

Thank you to my mum and dad for your continuing
support, encouragement and trust. To my dad, who
has taught me to think like a mathematician in
everyday life – N.S.

First published in Great Britain in 2022 by Wren & Rook

Copyright © Hodder & Stoughton Limited, 2022

HB ISBN: 978 1 5263 6196 7
PB ISBN: 978 1 5263 6198 1
E-book ISBN: 978 1 5263 6197 4
10 9 8 7 6 5 4 3 2 1

MIX
Paper from
responsible sources
FSC® C104740

Wren & Rook
An imprint of
Hachette Children's Group
Part of Hodder & Stoughton
Carmelite House
50 Victoria Embankment
London EC4Y 0DZ

An Hachette UK Company
www.hachette.co.uk
www.hachettechildrens.co.uk

Managing Editor: Liza Wilde
Senior Editor: Sadie Smith
Art Director: Laura Hambleton
Designer: Barbara Ward

Printed in China